Penguin Bloom

D0061464

For Sam

First published in Great Britain in 2017 by
Canongate Books Ltd, 14 High Street,
Edinburgh EH1 1TE

www.canongate.co.uk

2

First published in Australia and New Zealand in 2016
by HarperCollinsPublishers Australia Pty Limited
Level 13, 201 Elizabeth Street, Sydney, NSW 2000, Australia
Unit D1, 63 Apollo Drive, Rosedale, Auckland 0632, New Zealand

British Library Cataloguing-in-Publication Data

A catalogue record for the book is available
on request from the British Library

ISBN 9781782119814

Printed and bound in Great Britain by Clays Ltd, Elcograf S.p.A.

Penguin Bloom

The odd little bird who saved a family

Cameron Bloom & Bradley Trevor Greive

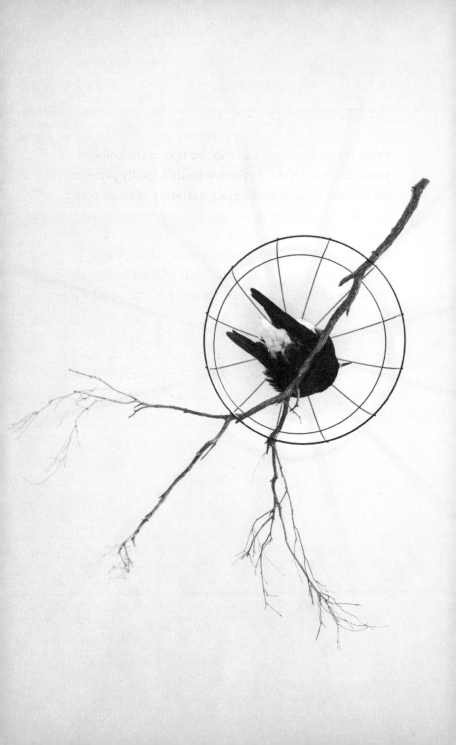

Acknowledgements

From the first images and scribbled text to the polished prose, finished layout, environmentally friendly paper and the exquisitely neat binding, a great many talented people have poured their heart and soul into the beautiful book you now hold in your hands.

Cameron Bloom and Bradley Trevor Greive would especially like to thank Brigitta Doyle of ABC Books, whose genuine and enduring passion for this story has truly made all the difference.

They would also like to express their deep personal and professional gratitude to Simon 'M' Milne of HarperCollins Publishers Australia, and Sir Albert Zuckerman of Writers House, New York, for their wisdom and support.

Family

As people know in black Africa and indigenous America, your
family is your entire village with all its inhabitants, living or dead.
Your relatives aren't only human.
Your family also speaks to you in the crackling of the fire,
in the murmur of running water,
in the breathing of the forest,
in the voices of the wind,
in the fury of thunder,
in the rain that kisses you
and in the birdsong that greets your footsteps.

Eduardo Galeano

Translation by Mark Fried

Preface

Our story is deeply painful to share, but it is also beautiful and true.

Just know that when I tell you about the tears, the anger and the longing, I am also talking about love.

We have laughed till we cried and we have wept ourselves to sleep, for that is the nature of love.

Love hurts.

Love heals.

Prologue

I fell in love with Sam while eating a pie. She was wearing faded jeans, a white t-shirt and a blue apron dusted with flour; there was even a dab of flour on the tip of her nose. She was small, fearless, and cute as hell.

Sam worked at her parents' Newport Beach bakery on weekends and holidays while completing her nursing degree at the University of Technology in Sydney. Despite a heavy class schedule and long commute, she nonetheless lit up the shop whenever she was behind the front counter. I don't know where she found the energy.

Sam grew up a tomboy. As a kid she was shy and quiet, but she never sat still; probably couldn't. When she wasn't at school or riding her skateboard, she was cleaning houses or babysitting to earn pocket money; even as a teenager her goal was financial independence. Always smiling and hilariously stubborn, Sam was her father's daughter through and through. She was raised to love hard work, abhor idleness, and laugh at pain. To her, a busy day is a good day and Panadol is for wimps.

I can't imagine what Sam's father thought when he realised I had a crush on his daughter. I had no interest in university and left school as soon as I could. At thirteen I'd picked up my dad's old camera and, from that moment on, I knew exactly what my calling was. Three years later I won a surf photography contest for which I received forty dollars and six rolls of film. That's all that was needed for a cocky Australian teenager to believe he was destined to be the next Max Dupain.

Whether I was learning my trade in the studio, printing images in a darkroom or out on assignment, almost every day would begin and end on a surfboard. It was no coincidence that my favourite break was directly across the road from the Surfside Pie Shop whenever Sam was working there. Having memorised her schedule I would ride my last wave to the beach and make a beeline for the bakery. I'd order a hot beef and mushroom pie, followed by a custard tart and small talk. Then I would stay to eat my scrumptious purchases – dripping wet in my board shorts, teeth chattering, my feet covered in sand – and talk to Sam for as long as she would put up with me, often till closing time.

When my shorts were dry and I was feeling especially brave, I would sidle up to Sam and sit next to her on the counter top, grinning like an idiot. Her dad would be baking in the rear, red-faced and furious in the heat of the giant ovens. His bloodshot eyes implied that open flirting would be dangerous – but I soon learned this was largely due to a flour allergy and that, despite his rock-cake exterior, he was actually a cream puff and very sympathetic to young love. I first knew I had a real chance with Sam when she gave me the unsold sausage rolls and lamingtons that would have otherwise been thrown out. At this point my dog, Bundy, loved Sam almost as much as I did.

Sam was never your average beach girl. When her friends gushed about local gossip, movie stars and Byron Bay, Sam spoke of medical science, books she'd enjoyed and her plans to visit West Africa when she graduated. Apart from being fun and beautiful there was something special about Sam that I found hard to define – though barely five feet in heels, she exuded a quiet strength; I felt energised by her love of life and warmed by her presence. She didn't always have much to say and never drew attention to herself, but she had an unspoken confidence that made you believe she could do anything she set her mind to. Something I now know to be absolutely true.

We were both nineteen when we went on our first date. After a drink or two at the Newport Arms Hotel, I worked up the courage to let Sam seize the initiative and invite me to a party at Bilgola Beach. And that was it. Sam was my first, last and only serious girlfriend – I knew I'd found the love of my life.

Our wedding was simple. Close friends and family squeezed into our backyard around a fancy chuppah that we'd borrowed from a wedding I had photographed a few weeks earlier. Apart from how stunning Sam looked, I can't forget the incredible flowers and also the giant chocolate mudcake baked by Sam's dad who, with tears of joy, embraced me as a son. Before the festivities got out of control I surprised my bride by arranging a Maori dance company to perform traditional songs and a haka which, I have to admit, was a bit weird seeing as neither of us were from New Zealand, and yet it was also somehow perfect. Hearing Sam's delighted laughter made me want to marry her all over again.

Sam began her nursing career on the neurosurgical ward of the Royal Prince Alfred Hospital in Camperdown. Our first home was a pocket-sized 1900s terrace house in Sydney's inner west, though we never lost our coastal roots and frequently made the cross-town pilgrimage to the beach. Besides our love of the ocean, we shared a passion for travel. Whenever we could get away to explore the world and experience new cultures we would shrug on backpacks and set off for parts unknown.

We didn't have much money, but that didn't matter as neither of us cared for luxury resorts or packaged holidays. Sam and I are outdoors people – we prefer dusty trails to city streets, mud huts to museums, and street food to fine dining. To us, a ballroom lit by glittering chandeliers seems dull compared to a night sky filled with unknown constellations.

By the time we celebrated our tenth anniversary we'd trekked around the Mediterranean and beyond. Sam's dream to visit Africa was realised five times over, and included journeys through Morocco, Senegal, Mali, Mauritania, Burkino Faso, Ivory Coast, Ghana, Togo, Botswana and Ethiopia. We also explored the Middle East and set foot in places that are now completely off-limits to tourists. The further we went, the more deeply we fell in love. The more deeply we fell in love, the further we wanted to travel.

Many of my most precious and enduring memories were made with Sam during these rugged and joyful wanderings. I'll never forget our pre-dawn climb up Mount Nemrut in Turkey; riding Arabian horses to the Step Pyramid of Djoser, the first pyramid ever built in Egypt; or standing together beside the ramparts of Fakhr-al-Din al-Maani Castle, perched high above the Bronze Age ruins of Palmyra in Syria.

It wasn't all about lost cities and difficult terrain – during a week spent navigating the labyrinthine backstreets of Rome we ate handmade pasta till we thought we would burst. And then we ate some more. Exotic flavours and ethnic cuisine have always been things we loved and these played a very important part in our lives – after all, food brought us together in the first place.

Sam and I felt blessed to share these extraordinary experiences and only wished that our children and grandchildren might one day enjoy a similar opportunity. We never imagined we'd stop travelling, indeed we hoped to return to Africa as soon as possible, but life had bigger plans for us, plans conceived in a flimsy tent on the plains of Kenya. I was over the moon when Sam found out she was pregnant. Adorably stoic with her enormous belly, almost as big around as she was tall, Sam pottered about the house like a determined beetle.

Her first pregnancy was the hardest. Sam wanted a natural birth, but after twenty-two hours in labour things were not going well. It became clear our baby was suffering foetal distress and the obstetrics team scrambled to perform an emergency caesarean. In the rush to deliver our child safely the spinal epidural failed and Sam felt the surgeon's scalpel slice into her tight flesh. This had to be agonising and yet somehow she bore it. Sam's face turned deathly pale but she just gripped my hand tightly and would not cry out. I don't believe anything on this earth could have eased her terrible pain but seeing the tiny, perfect face of our baby boy, Rueben.

After such a harrowing experience I would have understood if Sam had not wanted to endure childbirth ever again, but she loved being a mother and wanted a larger family. Amazingly, when it came time to deliver our second son, Noah, Sam was so calm and positive she chose to ride with me to the hospital on the back of our silver Vespa – an array of shocked and smiling faces greeted us as we puttered into the maternity car park. Two years later Sam and I welcomed little Oliver into the world, and our family was complete.

By now we had moved to Sydney's Northern Beaches, back to where we both grew up. Sam stepped away from full-time nursing to raise our three boisterous sons and the advent of digital photography meant I could work from home and be a hands-on dad. It was heaven.

With three semi-wild boys to wrangle we couldn't trot around the globe like we used to, but we didn't slow down either. Sam and I surfed and swam at the beach as often as possible. Sam also went skateboarding, running and mountain bike riding, plus she played soccer and, as if that wasn't enough, she regularly worked out at the local gym. It's no surprise that the boys all took after their mum, each becoming avid multi-sport athletes before they could even lace up their running shoes – our garage was cluttered with BMX bikes, surfboards, skateboards, muddy football boots and rugby balls.

As birthday parties came and went, we became increasingly excited about the boys being old enough for us to share our love of adventure travel with them. We dreamt up all manner of international itineraries but we were so busy trying to keep our home in order, stay on top of work, and supervise our children's education and activities that we began to wonder if we'd ever see the inside of an airplane again. But when Sam's father died, we knew that we simply had to make the time. Losing such a beloved role model hit us hard and reminded us that, as parents, we needed to create as many happy memories with our children as we possibly could.

Egypt was our first choice. We wanted to show the boys that ancient history was living history. Sadly, conditions had deteriorated since we were last in the Middle East – it was no place for foreign travellers, let alone those accompanied by young children. We decided our first major family adventure should be closer to home, so we chose Thailand, a fascinating country about which we had heard many wonderful things.

We made our way to Phuket, which, to our surprise, is now the most popular beach destination in Southeast Asia. The locals were lovely and the beaches were beautiful, but the Thai culture we wanted our children to experience was all but invisible within what was effectively an international party town for teenage backpackers. Having had such high expectations Sam and I were dispirited but by no means defeated. We were very happy for other tourists to have their fun, but we hadn't spent ten hours on a plane so that our impressionable boys could eat cheeseburgers and snicker at offensive novelty t-shirts.

After a refreshing dip in the Andaman Sea to compose ourselves, we considered our options over a meal of chicken satay and rice. Before the sun had set we'd planned our escape. We would head to Chiang Mai and beyond, some fifteen hundred kilometres to the north. There we would seek out Thailand's indigenous hill tribes in the mountainous borderlands of Myanmar and Laos. On the way we planned to make stops along the coast, both to relax and to experience authentic rural Thai life.

The Bloom family bundled into a minivan the next morning and drove east–northeast on the Phetkasem Road, the longest highway in Thailand. Six hours later we had crossed the Malay Peninsula to the South China Sea and pulled into a small, coastal village on the Gulf of Thailand just in time for dinner. It was perfect.

At first light the following day we woke up eager to explore. Other than swaying coconut palms, the beach was empty. The water was calling us so we all dived in and spent the next three hours laughing and splashing about like happy fools – for Sam and I the sense of joy and relief was palpable. Thailand was turning out to be the dream family adventure we'd hoped it would be.

As the boys wrestled and clowned around in the shore-break, Sam slipped on a turquoise t-shirt and a pair of black board shorts over her bikini. Following her lead the rest of us towelled off, threw on shirts and thongs, and strolled over to the hotel's reception desk where I made enquiries about renting bicycles. Our leisurely goal for the day was simply to pedal through the countryside to get a better sense of where we were and what was on offer.

No one had eaten and perhaps it was the heat and humidity but, despite our early start and active morning, we all felt thirsty rather than hungry. The sweet, elderly lady at the open-air bar near the front desk offered to make us fresh juice from hand-picked tropical fruit and crushed ice. It was just what we needed. The boys chose combinations of pineapple, mango and coconut water; the latter primarily so they could watch the petite Thai grandmother deftly wield a massive machete to split open the coconut husk and brittle shell beneath. Sam and I both ordered fresh papaya juice with a dash of kaffir lime. In an instant the sea salt was washed out of my mouth. I don't think I'd ever tasted anything so refreshing.

While slurping contentedly, we looked across the courtyard and spotted a spiral stairway leading to a rooftop viewing deck, so we headed on up to get our bearings as we finished our juice. We were delighted to find that this elevated vantage, just over two storeys high, offered uninterrupted views in every direction. Sam and the boys surveyed the endless stretch of sand for any promising surf breaks – a rarity in the Gulf. Turning away from the beach, I realised we were far more isolated than I had initially thought, surrounded by coconut and pineapple plantations, as well as several drowsy-looking water buffalo.

By now it was almost eleven and everything felt hot and still. Other than a proudly dishevelled rooster flying up to a perch in the branches of a colossal rubber tree nearby, almost nothing was moving. I spotted a Buddhist temple glinting and shimmering in the distance, so I took a few photos and made a mental note of where we should ride our bicycles after lunch, or perhaps later in the day when things had cooled down.

And then time stopped.

I heard a horrendous crash of broken bells, a violent ringing of metal striking stone.

Sam had leant against the safety fence – parallel rows of steel poles bolted to concrete pillars via sturdy-looking timber posts that, unknown to us, were riddled with dry rot. The barrier collapsed beneath her and it was the spinning poles sparking against the hard, blue, cement tiles six metres below that jarred my ears and spun me around by my head.

Startled by the fence giving way, Sam was pulled off balance. She stood poised on the edge for a seemingly infinite sliver of time – leaning back over the void at an impossible angle, her slim arms waving wildly, fingers extended as if to find purchase in the air and take flight.

And then she was gone.

She didn't scream. I never heard her hit the ground. My ears were roaring with dreadful silence. My mind went blank, all thoughts but one instantly erased in a blinding flash of fear and horror. I dropped my juice and ran to the edge. Looking down was more terrible than I could have imagined. Sam lay twisted on the tiles twenty feet below.

She was utterly still.

Time and space seemed to fold into itself. Suddenly I was kneeling by Sam's side. She was unconscious but alive. Barely.

The violent impact had thrown off her red thongs, and her sunglasses had also vanished. Her eyelids were not quite closed and I could just glimpse the lower whites of her eyes. This was unnerving enough, but then I saw the hideous bony bulge in the middle of her back, an angry misshapen lump the size of my fist pushing through her t-shirt and I feared the worst.

Sam had bitten through her tongue – her clenched teeth were stained red – and each ragged, gasping breath was a weak and bubbling spectral wheeze. I tried opening her mouth to clear her airway but her jaw was locked shut. I ripped off my shirt and crumpled it into a small pillow, then I tried to tilt her face gently to the side and into the recovery position. But as soon as my cupped hands cradled her head they immediately felt warm and wet. Blood was seeping through her blonde hair everywhere I looked. Her head had been split open in two different directions. No matter where I put my hands, no matter where I parted her hair or how firmly I held my blood-soaked shirt against her head as a compress, I could not stem the bleeding or find the edges of the jagged wounds that were its source. I glanced down and saw Sam's angelic face at the centre of an ever-expanding crimson halo as her lifeblood pooled onto the concrete. My heart emptied of hope.

I shouted for help. I tried desperately and feebly to comfort my unconscious wife. I shouted for an ambulance. I screamed for help again. I needed someone, anyone, to hold my boys back; I didn't want them to see their mother like this. But when I looked up, all three were standing right next to me; silent, ashen-faced.

Noah made no sound, but hot tears were streaming down his cheeks. The horror was too much for little Oli, who doubled over and vomited. Rueben, the eldest, did his best to be brave but, when he tried to speak, his voice came out a ghostly whisper: 'Is Mummy going to die?' To this day I can't remember what I said in reply. Or if I said anything at all.

Fellow tourists and Thai locals rushed in; some corralled and comforted the youngest boys, while others dropped down beside me to do whatever I asked of them. Rueben sprinted to the front desk to call an ambulance. Within twenty minutes, paramedics arrived and took control – Sam was strapped to a long, orange spinal board and ferried to the ambulance. I stumbled after my beloved wife, wanting to do anything and everything I could to save her, but capable of doing nothing.

Sam would remain lashed to that orange plank for the next three days, as she was rolled in and out of emergency rooms, and made the long and difficult journey from the local medical centre to a far larger hospital closer to Bangkok. She drifted in and out of semi-consciousness – she was in terrible pain and would sleepily fumble with the restraining straps and try to remove the mask and tubes that were keeping her alive. During fleeting moments when comprehension dawned she would try to call out my name and then start to cry.

A team of surgeons wanted to operate straight away, but Sam's blood pressure was far too unstable to survive an operation. And so we waited. And waited. I was told there was only 'a chance she might pull through'.

The consul from the Australian Embassy drove down from the capital to help me look after the boys and install them in a nearby hotel. At some point I showered and changed, attempted to feed myself and get some sleep, but Sam's critical condition and suffering were all-consuming. I wanted to keep my eyes on my wife at all times, afraid that I would miss her final breath, terrified that I wouldn't.

When finally she was wheeled out of the operating theatre, and her bed was parked in a high-tech life support bay in the intensive care unit, I received a full report: Sam's skull was fractured in several places, and her brain was bleeding and badly bruised. Both lungs had ruptured and one had completely collapsed due to her chest cavity filling with blood. There wasn't an organ in her body that hadn't been battered, and her spine was shattered at T6 and T7, just below her shoulder blades.

After resurfacing from the anaesthetic, Sam was able to breathe on her own, which was a huge relief, but she still couldn't feel her legs. However, the bruising on her back was so severe that we were told it was likely she was suffering from spinal shock and that nerve signals would return gradually as the swelling receded over six to eight weeks.

Although her tongue was mending, her frightful head injuries caused constant migraine headaches that made it even harder for her to talk. When the boys were first allowed to visit and they saw her badly swollen face, Noah froze, thinking his mother was dead. When at last she finally spoke, it was not to complain or seek our pity, but to repeatedly apologise for ruining our family holiday. Sam's selflessness and courage were extraordinary, but not infectious – I couldn't hold back my tears and soon we all were weeping.

Weeks crawled by with little to no sign of improvement. Sam had lost her sense of taste and smell, and she had no reflex response below the ominous bruising on her back. But she stayed positive and refused pain medication as often as she could stand it, hoping to feel the first tingling that indicated her recovery had begun in earnest. When her condition was deemed stable for travel, she was flown back to a Sydney hospital where she waited patiently for better news. It never came.

In my absence a callous doctor brusquely told Sam that it was obvious she'd never walk again. My brave wife was devastated. How she managed to commit herself to the rehabilitation process after this ruinous blow I do not know. But she did. With a vengeance.

It was seven months before Sam was released from the spinal ward. The boys and I were beside ourselves to have her home but, for all the bright smiles on show, each of us felt heartbroken and afraid. The veneer of celebration barely concealed our sense of hopelessness.

Sam did her best to seem upbeat for our sake. But we could see her struggling. Every day presented her with a battle she couldn't win. No longer able to follow her heart or commit her restless energy to immediate purpose, she sat at the edge of family life, watching, wishing. Sam quietly mourned the loss of her former self; she would cry herself to sleep and cry herself awake. Whenever the boys came in to see her she would rally; however, I could sense that, for the first time, her inner strength was beginning to fail. She was no longer the force of nature she had always been. Her smiles grew less radiant and less frequent. The time it took her to emerge from our bedroom each morning grew longer and longer. She didn't want to wake up any more.

Sam felt broken and utterly adrift. I saw the light in her eyes grow dim. I knew she was withdrawing from this world.

That such a fiercely free and passionate spirit could now be anchored beyond our love by pain and a steel chair was too much for us to bear.

I sought advice and support wherever I could, but nothing seemed to help.

I was slowly but surely losing the love of my life.

And then Penguin arrived.

'Hope' is the thing with feathers

Emily Dickinson

Penguin Bloom

Angels come in all shapes and sizes.

Penguin was just a small, wobbly-headed magpie chick when my son Noah found her lying in the car park next to his grandmother's house.

Gusting onshore winds had tossed her out of her nest, some twenty metres up a towering Norfolk Island pine, and she had tumbled, spun and bounced her way through the branches to fall heavily onto the cold asphalt.

One wing was hanging limply by her side and, though too battered to move a great deal, she was extremely lucky to survive such a horrendous fall.

But she wasn't out of danger yet. Without immediate care the shaky little chick would have died within hours.

Our family had witnessed enough tragedy for one lifetime and we were not going to sit idly by. Sam let Noah pick up the little bird and, with grandmother at the wheel, they sped for home.

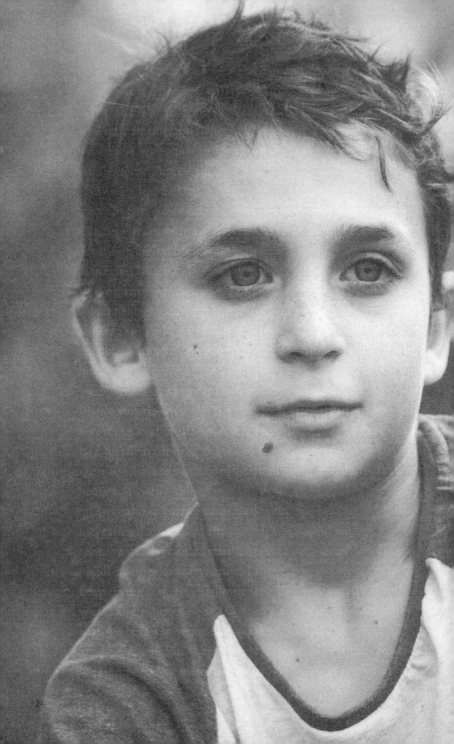

Unable to find an animal rescue shelter that would take in an injured baby bird, Sam and I decided that we would care for her until she was fully healed and became strong enough to fend for herself. If we failed, then we would lay her to rest in the backyard. Either way, she was staying with us.

The boys immediately named her Penguin, after her black-and-white plumage, and that was that.

Our three sons suddenly had a baby sister. Miss Penguin Bloom.

We didn't own a cage and we weren't inclined to get one. Penguin was a wild bird and we didn't want her to grow up to be any other way. We made a simple nest out of an old cane laundry basket and lined this with soft cotton fabric to keep her warm.

It is not easy to look after any sick or injured creature, and this is especially true of a baby bird – as we soon found out. Our little girl was quite a handful. Caring for Penguin, especially during those first few weeks, was a massive commitment.

Initially Penguin had to be fed every two hours. Noah, Oli and Rueben took turns with feeding duty before and after school, while Sam and I took over resident chef and nanny duties throughout the rest of the day.

But while getting Penguin to eat, drink and rest was a real victory, her recovery remained touch and go.

Though her damaged wing turned out not to be broken, she was severely weakened by her fall and prone to illness.

There were many days when Penguin refused her food and appeared so listless we thought we might lose her.

Some evenings, as we tucked her into bed, we wondered if she would survive the night.

Despite the setbacks, we continued to do all we could for the smallest member of our family. Over time, with a great deal of patience and a whole lot of love, Penguin grew in stature and confidence.

As an avian toddler her wingspan wasn't especially impressive, and she often resembled a manic fluff-ball with a beak, but we occasionally caught glimpses of the proud airborne goddess she was destined to become.

As with most adolescents, Penguin went through an awkward phase. When her adult feathers started to come through, she entered what we called her 'Goth period'.

But she never stopped being fabulous in her own weird and wonderful way, and we certainly didn't love her any less.

Like so many younger sisters she soon learned how to drive her big brothers crazy and somehow get away with it. But they always made up in the end and remained the very best of friends.

Sam and I had to admit, it was quite adorable watching the 'kids' grow up together.

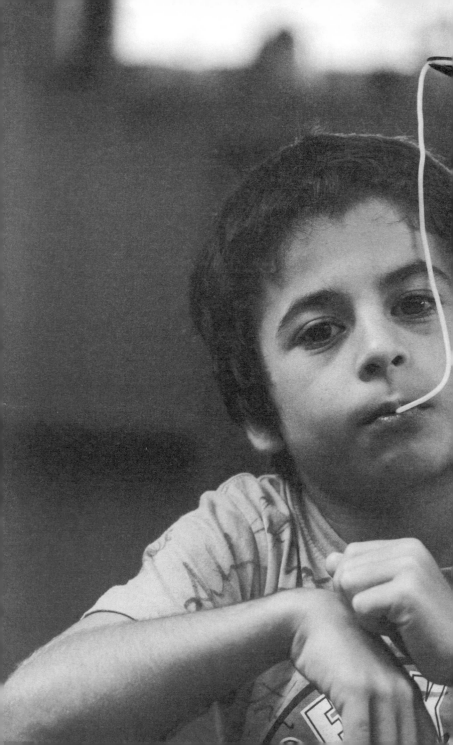

Penguin's strength increased, as did her curiosity. We never locked her inside any kind of enclosure so she was always able to go anywhere she pleased.

It didn't take long before she started to forage for her own food in the backyard to supplement her diet, and it was clear she was becoming more and more independent.

Despite being free to leave, Penguin still chose to sleep inside the house. We were happy that she liked living with us, but we also wanted her to follow her natural instincts and develop magpie-appropriate behaviours.

Though, to be honest, we really had no idea what those might be.

For Penguin's own good, she needed to spend a lot more time outdoors. Her long-term health and wellbeing depended on her being able to look after herself in her natural environment, and playing video games and watching movies could hardly be considered adequate preparation for this important transition.

Also, it must be said, there is no such thing as potty-training a magpie – at least so far as we could tell. After Penguin added her signature flourish to the furniture, carpet, bedspreads, curtains, hats, television and computers for the umpteenth time, we decided she was old enough to get her own apartment.

This was not an especially popular decision.

Fortunately there is a large frangipani tree in our yard that Penguin has always seemed to like, so that became her new principal residence.

She was still very close to the house in case she ever felt inclined to drop by – which she often did. Even so, it was a difficult time for Penguin. It wasn't easy for us either, watching her make her way into the unknown.

We worried about her constantly.

And with good reason.

Magpies can be fiercely territorial, and sometimes Penguin would be beaten up by a gang of local bully-birds who would knock her to the ground and then scratch and claw at her, snapping at her feathers and pecking at her eyes.

Our brave girl held her own, but it was truly awful seeing her injured and in pain.

And it was doubly heartbreaking watching her realise that such viciousness was part of her world.

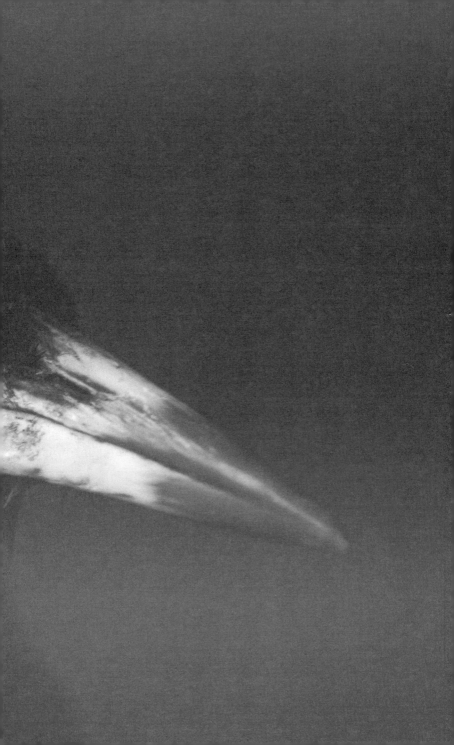

To her great credit, Penguin never let her violent oppressors break her spirit. Australian magpies are known for their beautiful songs and Penguin is blessed with a wonderful voice. She loves to sing and will do so for hours at a time.

Penguin always seems to know exactly when our boys will be walking home from school. As 3.30pm draws near, she positions herself in the orange tree at the edge of our property, waiting for them to come around the corner. As soon as she hears them approaching, she breaks out in song and the boys happily reply in their best, garbled magpie impersonation. They continue calling out to each other, again and again, in a joyful chorus of greeting.

Likewise, whenever Sam and I pull up in the driveway she lets out a loud, melodic warble to welcome us home. Then she flaps her wings and wiggles her tail feathers with excitement and prances to the front door to be let inside.

Keeping Penguin outside the house is a challenge we quite enjoy failing. Though she has moved out for good, Penguin will always be a welcome visitor in our home – something she seems to have taken for granted.

We try our best to make sure she sleeps on her frangipani perch, but if we ever leave a window open she'll zip inside the house at sunrise, scamper down the hallway to one of the bedrooms like an overexcited velociraptor and leap onto the covers for a bonus sleep-in.

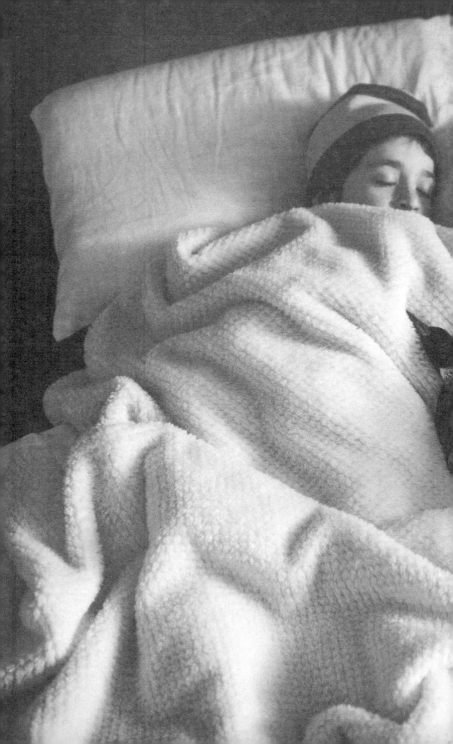

Penguin could not have arrived at a better time, by which I mean a more terrible time.

There are some things children should never have to see – and watching their mother be critically injured and almost die is very definitely one of those things.

When Sam finally came home, after more than half a year in hospital, she may have been out of immediate danger, but the painful reality of her condition had only just begun to sink in.

When I first carried her over the threshold it had been one of the happiest days of our lives. But this time around, carrying Sam from the car to our front door was one of the saddest occasions you could possibly imagine.

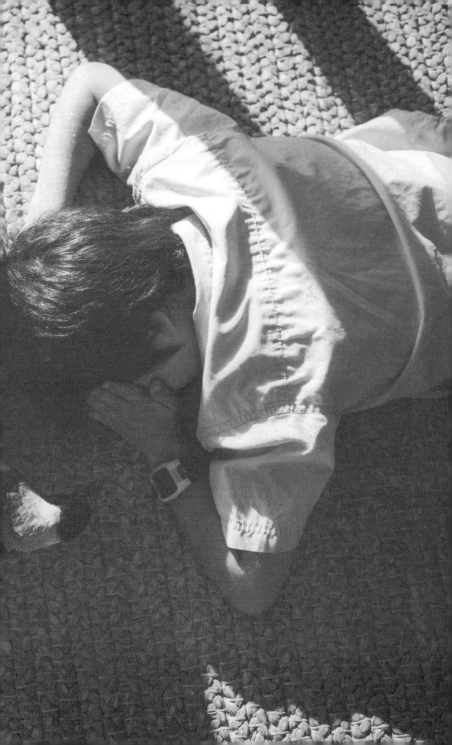

To be paralysed from the chest down means many things –
none of which are good.

Most immediately it means the loss of your legs and your
abdominal muscles. You cannot sit up, you cannot stand,
you cannot walk, you cannot skip, you cannot run.

You can no longer sense your connection to the earth.

You cannot feel the cool, wet grass between your toes, or
the hot summer sand beneath your feet, upon which you
will no longer leave a footprint.

You cannot feel the intimate connection with the one you
love above all others.

That part of your life is gone.

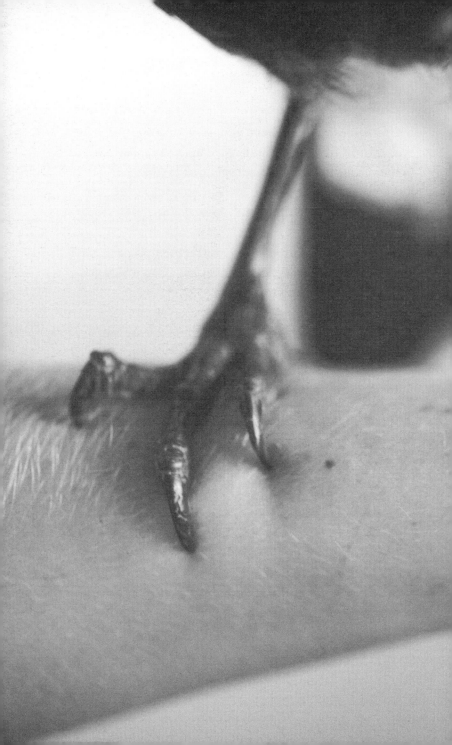

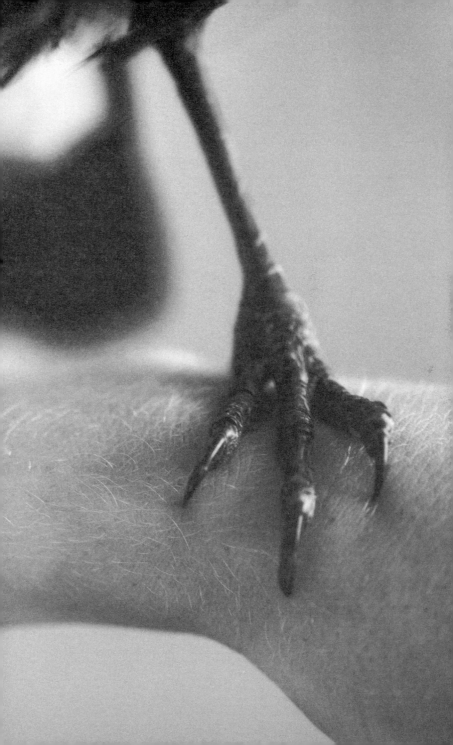

Wheelchair-bound, with two metal rods screwed into her fractured spine, Sam felt immobilised to the point of suffocation.

She couldn't bend down from her chair and she couldn't get up. Almost everything she wanted, everything she needed, was out of reach. To overextend without help nearby was to risk falling, being injured and becoming stuck.

To go anywhere or do anything she was wholly reliant upon wheels of steel and rubber, and other people's legs.

At all points in between, she was completely stranded.

Moving slowly and gingerly around the house in her wheelchair made the once familiar domestic terrain feel utterly foreign.

Even the smallest obstacle or surface change could block her path and leave her feeling isolated and imprisoned.

It didn't feel real.

We wanted to believe it was all just a bad dream.

That when we finally opened our eyes, things would be as they were before the accident.

But it wasn't a dream.

Sam was completely overwhelmed.

We all were.

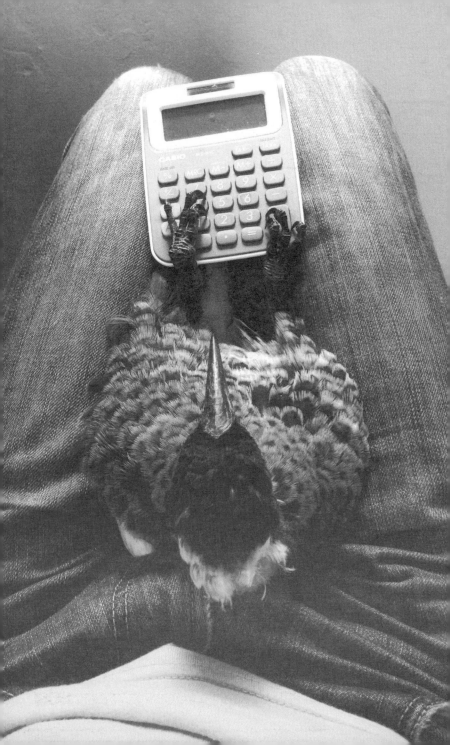

I cannot even begin to tabulate the cost of the accident to the family, or to Sam herself.

I don't mean in terms of time and money, though in that regard the drain was enormous – we relied on the generous support of friends and family to function effectively as parents, and to cope with the expense of remodelling the house to accommodate Sam's wheelchair.

I mean in terms of the terrible price we all had to pay, and keep paying every day – the great and small things no one could ever have anticipated that rapidly consumed Sam's will to live and exhausted the family's emotional reserves.

It is a myth that spinal cord injury victims feel no pain at the site of their break – which in Sam's case is in line with her heart – or within their affected limbs.

She suffered from unpredictable bursts of incredible agony: phantom pains dancing through her otherwise lifeless legs and feet, sudden rushes of bee-sting sensations along her break-line, and searing heat that spread throughout her lower back like tentacles of fire. She also endured frightening muscular spasms; her largely dormant torso muscles would violently contract, taking her breath away, and the muscles along her spine would cramp and twist painfully, as if rejecting the steel rods biting into her vertebrae.

Her injuries are such that she can never feel comfortable, regardless of the resting surface or her body position. This alone is enough to unravel anybody.

Even when Sam goes to bed she is denied the sweet relief afforded by a good night's sleep. I help her turn over three times before dawn in order to maintain her circulation and to prevent pressure sores.

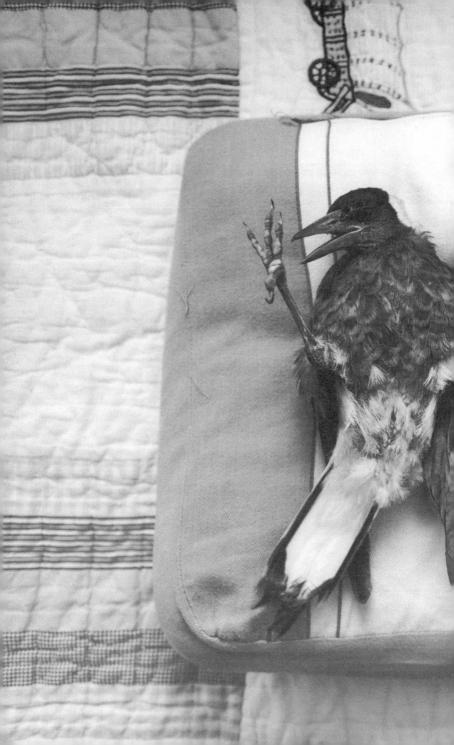

Sam's constant physical struggle was compounded by the mental anguish of not being able to do things around the house that she had always taken for granted. Countless domestic chores we used to share that she never imagined she'd miss, such as cooking and cleaning, were now extremely difficult. Something as simple as dashing down to the local shops to pick up a few groceries was downright impossible without help.

In and of themselves such things might not seem that important, but, taken together, this endless barrage of what she perceived to be personal failures started to destroy Sam's self-image as a wife and mother, and as a strong, independent woman.

Always being supervised, examined or assisted, Sam's personal space was constantly being violated. She no longer enjoyed any privacy.

Every mundane activity common to humanity had the potential to be humiliating.

Getting dressed each morning became a form of torture.

To add insult to grievous injury, residual brain damage, though relatively minor, had robbed Sam of her sense of taste.

For someone whose love of flavour and epicurean discovery was a life passion, this seemed like a very sick joke.

As did the fact that Sam's sense of smell was likewise diminished to the degree that the only fragrance she could distinguish was fish.

Even Sam had to admit this was excellent material for a black comedy.

But laughing at such an absurdly cruel twist of fate didn't make daily life any more enjoyable.

Far from sustaining her, memories of happier times towered over the present, making everything she did feel small and pitiful.

Sam felt like a spectator watching from the sidelines, stuck in the cheapest seats imaginable.

Seeing other people free from pain and having fun brought her no pleasure.

Quite the opposite, in fact.

While she seldom showed it, almost every happy or beautiful thing Sam saw filled her heart with rage – she was constantly angry with herself for every single thing she ever did that led to her being in this miserable position.

As Sam fixated on her changed appearance and loss of function, her perspective distorted. She saw herself as broken and embarrassing, and found it hard to accept that anyone could see her as otherwise.

Such intense feelings of pain, fury and regret could not possibly be contained – she presented a brave face to the world, but she would weep in the bedroom and the shower where no one could witness her tears.

The emotional distance increased between Sam and everyone who loved her.

She didn't want anyone to see her like this.

She didn't want anyone to see her. Period.

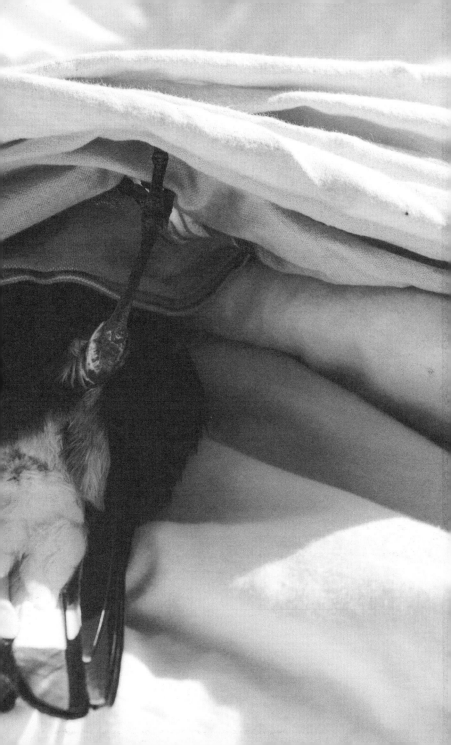

Endless gloom descended upon our once happy home.

Every day felt like a funeral.

Sam was staring into the abyss.

I don't know when she first considered suicide, but I know it was early on and that she thought of it often. Almost constantly.

Sam was enduring so much pain and mental anguish that I cannot blame her. I understood her fractured reasoning at the time. But to allow her dark thoughts to manifest as irrevocable action would have destroyed our young family. I couldn't bear the thought of losing her.

All I could do was tell her over and over how much I loved her, how much the boys loved her, how much we all needed her.

I knew her suffering was great, but I always believed her love for us was greater still.

And I was right.

Sam turned away from the darkness. She chose us.

Not because she lacked the courage to face oblivion, but because she had the far greater courage to live.

To be truly selfless and loving is the very opposite of weakness. And no one is as strong as my Sam.

She knew she had a very difficult road ahead and she faced it bravely.

She didn't shirk her rehabilitation, however much she hated it.

She soldiered on, day after day.

Sam did whatever she could to convince herself that her life was not over, even though, deep inside, she felt the opposite to be true.

She found some solace when listening to music.

And also enjoyed the escape afforded when reading.

But when your body craves physical relief, you can only listen to so much music and read so many books.

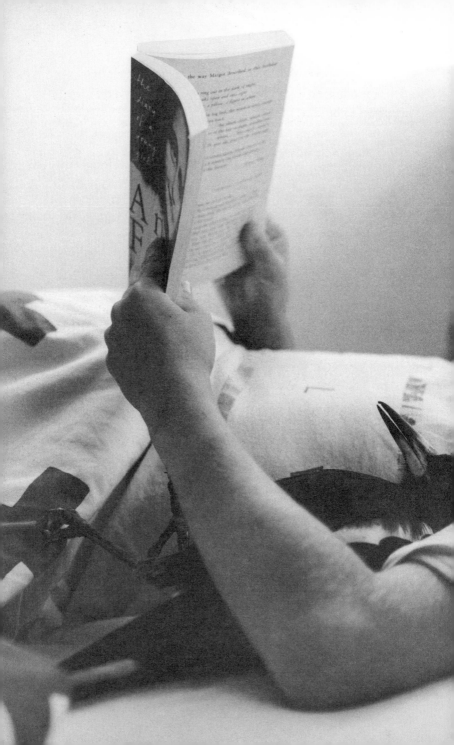

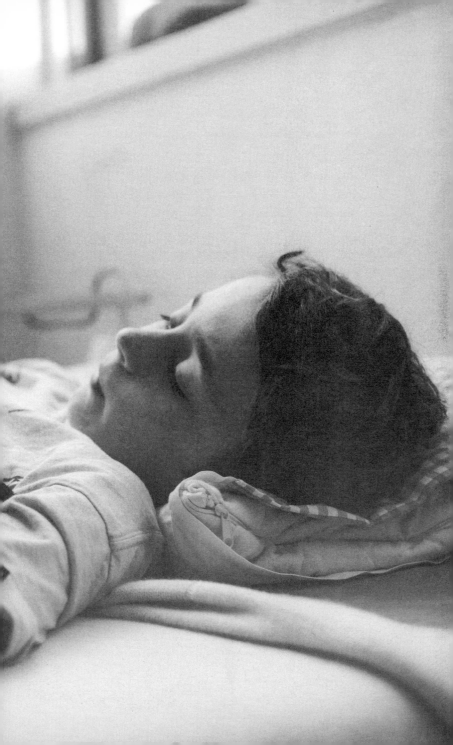

Our home certainly didn't lack for compassion.

But Sam struggled to come to terms with her disability at a level that we could neither relate to nor understand.

She didn't want our sympathy. She didn't want to be coddled. She didn't want anyone's pity or platitudes. She just wanted her old life back.

And that notion, the utterly gut-wrenching, soul-crushing feeling that your life has been stolen from you is something that you cannot hope to fathom unless you have been through it yourself.

Every terrible thing you have been through in your life up till that point pales in comparison or seems downright ridiculous. You don't even know where to begin. I know I didn't.

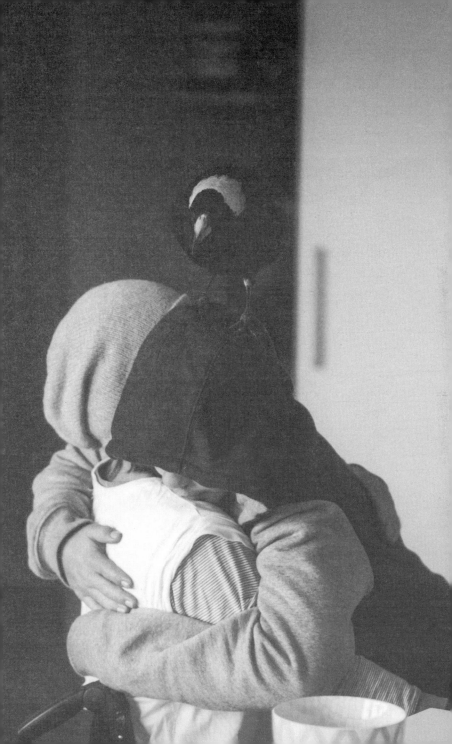

All I can say is that we never gave up.

We just kept trying to reach her.

We did whatever we could to bridge the emotional gulf between us.

We tried to find the balance between giving Sam space and being close by whenever she needed us.

We waited till she let us draw near.

We waited till she was ready to talk.

It was extremely hard for Sam to speak aloud the fears and regrets she was forced to live with. And then, when she did have something to say, we had almost nothing we could offer her in reply except that we loved her, that we would always love her, and that we would do whatever we could to help.

The best we could tell her was that the future would not be as bleak as she believed; that things were going to get better. Which, though certainly true and vaguely encouraging, as far as clichés go, fell well short of being inspiring.

All of which is to say, words failed us.

And this is where Penguin came into her own. She was our fearless ambassador of love and chief motivational officer.

When it came to taking an interest in her family's wellbeing, Penguin was as tender as a baby pea –

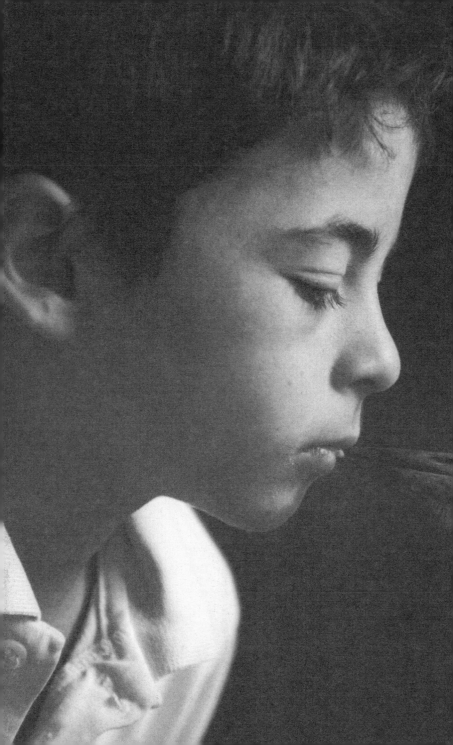

and as subtle as a black-and-white brick.

Penguin and Sam became inseparable.

One was always looking after the other.

When Penguin was weak and sickly, Sam would lovingly nurse her back to health.

And when Sam found it hard to get moving, Penguin would sing her energy levels up.

If Sam was inside, doing paperwork or writing in her private journal, Penguin would be there.

If Sam was outside, painting and enjoying the sunshine, Penguin would be there.

Penguin didn't just stay around for the fun and novel activities. She was fiercely loyal to Sam and would provide a melodic chirp of encouragement whenever anything proved more challenging than might have been expected.

During the most difficult moments, when Sam had to confront her disability directly, Penguin made sure Sam always received the best possible care.

It's the Australian way not to make a fuss about your problems, and perhaps it was also the result of having been a nurse herself for many years, but as a patient Sam was overly meek and polite. She never spoke up when she needed pain relief or extra attention, and was always prepared to accept an alarming degree of discomfort without complaint.

Penguin had no problem speaking up on Sam's behalf and, in doing so, this plucky bird helped Sam realise that her needs mattered, that she mattered, and that she was entitled to as much respect as anyone.

As Sam slowly came to terms with her strange new world, Penguin did the same. Always cheerful, always free of judgement, always there.

When training and physical therapy were over for the day, or the pain got too much to bear, they would lie outside beneath the sky.

I would often overhear the two of them having what sounded like long and in-depth conversations about what they were going through.

Sometimes Sam would speak softly to Penguin, sometimes Penguin would sing to Sam, and sometimes neither would make a sound for hours at a time.

I came to believe that each knew exactly what the other was feeling.

Their beautiful relationship could be defined as unlikely best friends, but it was deeper than that.

It was part mother and daughter, part nurse and patient.

And it was also two sister spirits, strong yet fragile, united by a single word: up.

Sam wanted to sit up straight, to stand tall on her own two feet, and Penguin wanted to fly above the trees and beyond the clouds.

Sam worked incredibly hard to build up her strength and stamina to regain as much of her independence as possible.

Every single day she would sweat out her demons with gym equipment or boxing mitts, or paddle her kayak for hours, often till her hands were blistered and bleeding.

She just wouldn't quit.

As her training progressed she finally saw a glimmer of daylight and, in time, her entire outlook brightened.

Small victories led to greater victories.

New challenges became new opportunities.

While Sam was very grateful for all the help she'd received, she was done with depending on others to keep her alive.

She was ready to start living on her own terms.

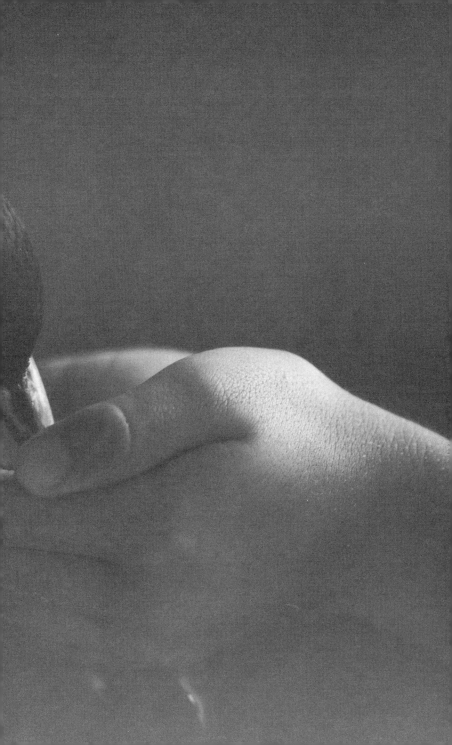

There were far fewer tears in the shower and a lot more laughter was heard around the house.

Making your way back to who you were and, in the process, learning who you really are can be a very difficult journey.

We undertook just such a journey together on the day before Christmas when I surprised Sam by taking her to a special place that she thought she would never see again: a rocky outcrop just beyond the historic Barrenjoey Lighthouse. This was where Sam and I used to go whenever we wanted to clear our heads. We would always leave for home feeling refreshed and so, in many ways, we regard this rocky platform as a spiritual haven.

The problem was that to get to Sam's rock you have to scramble along a steep, uneven, twisting path that takes you up an almost vertical 100-metre ascent. So I built a rustic-looking sedan chair out of bamboo and sofa cushions and a few of our closest and fittest friends helped me get Sam to the top.

As we gazed out to the horizon, we knew that reaching this rock was a symbol of our combined hopes and dreams, as well as our fears.

Life would be different. It wasn't going to be easy, and we would need the ongoing support of those close to us, but together we could go anywhere and accomplish anything.

Acknowledging the tremendous hardship Sam had faced, and the many challenges that lay ahead, made this moment of celebration rather quiet. But it was a genuine celebration nonetheless. Our tears were happy ones.

Penguin's defining moment came soon after.

With all respect to the Wright Brothers and their historic maiden voyage across the lower skies of North Carolina in 1903, for the Bloom family the most momentous first flight in history took place in our lounge room.

Our spirits soared on Penguin's black-and-white wings.

It was a moment of pure joy.

A Bloom family member had, at last, conquered gravity.

Caring for Penguin has changed our perspective on life, love and pretty much everything else. She has completely redefined what family means.

In the beginning we thought we were rescuing Penguin, but now we know this remarkable little bird has made us stronger, brought us closer as a family, given us countless reasons to smile and laugh during an extremely difficult time and, in doing so, helped us heal emotionally and physically.

So, in a very real way, Penguin rescued us.

It has been an extraordinary privilege to be part of
Penguin's life and to help her on her journey.

We have all learned so much from her along the way.

Looking at her now, with her bright eyes, powerful wings and lustrous feathers, it's hard to recall just how weak, crippled and near death she was when we first found her.

She is a completely different bird today.

Penguin's complete transformation is a daily reminder that we are not our past, no matter how traumatic or life-changing it might have been.

You don't have to be superhuman to survive the bad times and you can't always be at your best. But even when things look their worst, you can still feel positive about the future. Being optimistic is simply a choice made possible by being creative and proactive.

The means to achieving the breakthrough you need may be a lot closer than you think.

A happy ending begins with having faith in your own story, and looking for ways to create joy for yourself and others.

Time and time again Penguin showed us what a difference it can make just by giving our family and friends a reason to smile when they see us.

She also showed us how to be present.

There is nothing wrong with enjoying everything the modern world has to offer, but we must never let technology keep us from those we love.

Penguin constantly reminds us that we are all part of nature. And the more connected with nature we are, the happier we feel.

Penguin wakes up each morning believing the whole world is hers to enjoy. Which, I suppose, it is.

That, plus clean and well-groomed feathers, is her secret to rising above it all.

From cradling Penguin in my hands and holding Sam in my arms I can tell you that every nerve cell, every blood vessel, every atom of our being is precious.

But we are all so much more than the sum of our fragile parts.

We are all our journeys, hopes and dreams, clad in mortal wrapping paper.

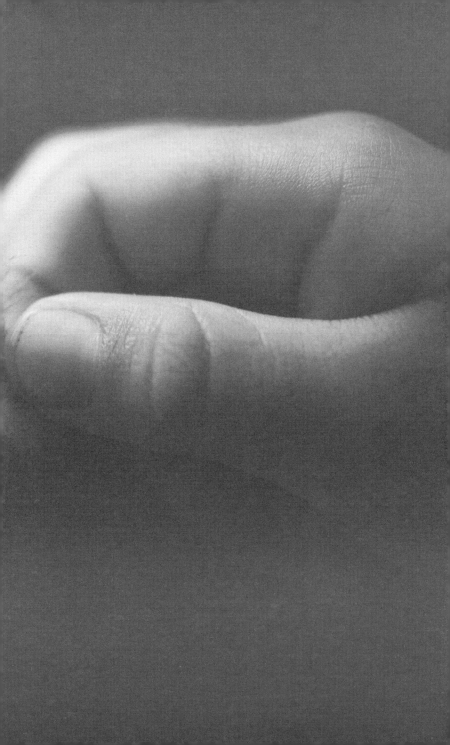

I have so often been told that life is short – but this didn't mean that much to me until the accident.

Now I realise we could have lost Sam and Penguin both, many times.

Just like that.

Their warm and vital presence is a powerful reminder that each and every moment matters.

So, on behalf of Penguin and Sam, I encourage you to say all the things you want to say.

Give voice to your heart.

Do all the things you want to do – don't waste a second. Lose yourself in the beauty of this world as often as possible.

Sam and I have always believed that love, togetherness and a spirit of discovery are the keys to enjoying life – Penguin proved this to be absolutely true.

Most importantly, Penguin taught us that helping others feel better is the easiest and best way to help yourself feel better.

She showed us there is so much more love in the world than we could possibly imagine.

Regardless of how bad things get, compassion, friendship and support can come from the most unexpected places.

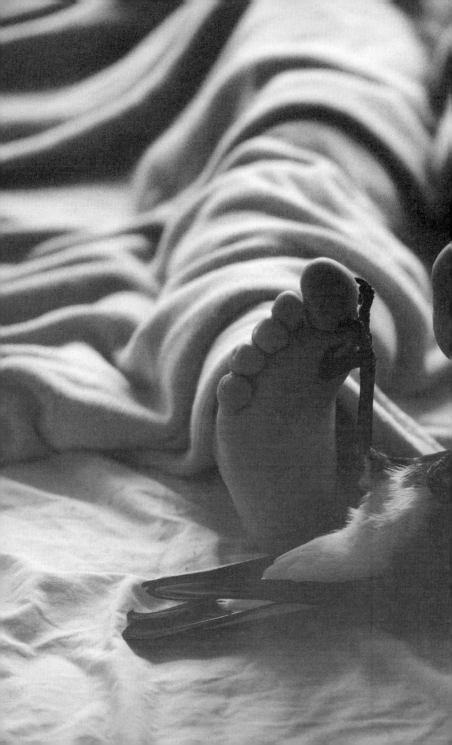

And no matter how lost, lonely, defeated or damaged we feel, accepting the love of others and loving them in return, to whatever degree we can, will help to make us whole again.

I am not the arbiter of wonders. All my life I have tried to capture the extraordinary with a crystal lens, and still I have not seen anything that helps me understand the why – only the what, when, where and how beautifully or cruelly our fate unfolds.

It is certainly not my place to know the unknowable and, in any case, I would always choose love over peace of mind.

And I have love.

As great a love as any man has known.

I may never accept that Sam's accident was part of any divine plan; her suffering is too great for me to believe such things.

But that she lived when so many others might have died, and that Penguin fell from the heavens when we needed her most – my heart tells me that if these were not miracles, then the Bloom family is still blessed beyond reason.

I am immensely grateful for our three brave and beautiful boys. Brothers by birth, friends by choice – in the face of tragedy and confusion they did not let anger and bitterness drive them apart, but instead stood by each other and responded with kindness and compassion.

They will never know how much their love and courage has meant to their mother and me, how they lifted us up when we could not rise on our own.

I am so thankful for the truly remarkable woman I am privileged to call my wife.

Sam's strength is the foundation upon which our home is built.

More than that, she is the most beautiful human being I have ever met.

Her natural grace, sense of humour, humility and heroic determination make everyone she comes in contact with want to be a better person.

Especially me.

I feel incredibly proud of us, as a family, and I am excited about what our future holds.

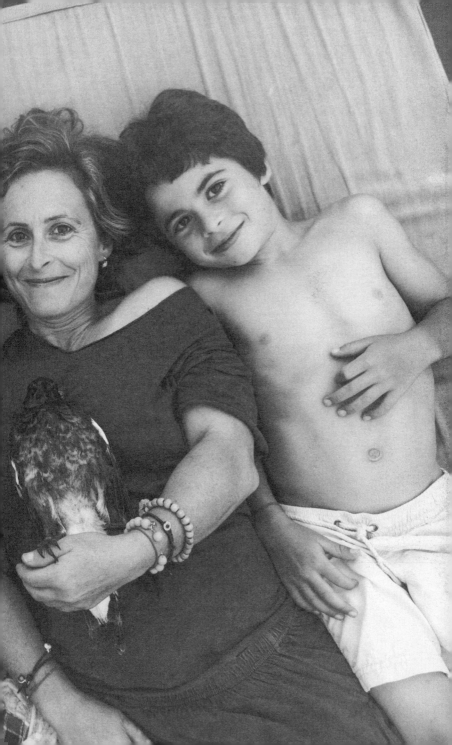

And I thank God for that crazy little bird.

Like I said – angels come in all shapes and sizes.

Epilogue

A lot has happened since Penguin first became a part of our family.

Sam has gone from strength to strength. Not only has she become far more independent, but she also has found ways to manage her constant physical pain and the corrosive depression that threatened to consume her.

The daily boost provided by the love and support that Sam receives from Penguin, our three boys and me cannot be overstated. But we also acknowledge that Sam's love of the water proved central to her progress and, best of all, has led her to a new life passion.

Kayaking is so much more than a change of scenery or a mere workout. It is the means by which Sam can escape the confines of her wheelchair and the static nature of a life lived between one assisted transition and the next. So much of Sam's time is spent waiting for others to help her in some way or other, but that ends abruptly at the water's edge – once she is in her boat, she is free to glide. When Sam picks up a paddle, she is in absolute control of where she is and what she is doing and, in that moment, she is once again her own person.

Not long after coming home, Sam joined the Manly Warringah Kayak Club and teamed up with coach Gaye Hatfield, who immediately spotted her potential. It wasn't easy to master a racing kayak using only her arms for balance and power but, once again, Sam used her father's sheer bloody-mindedness to positive effect.

Within a short time she was ready to participate in club events, where she surprised everyone with her speed, including herself. As her times dropped she progressed to more serious competition and within twelve months she was the fastest female KL1 paddler in Australia. When Sam claimed her second national title, and posted the eighth fastest time in the world that year, the sport's top national selectors were paying close attention. In March 2015, Sam was named a member of the Australian Paracanoe Team and joined the elite squad headed to the Canoe Sprint World Championships in Milan later that year.

Sam then worked harder than ever, undertaking six paddling sessions and three gym sessions every week. She also travelled to Queensland with the national team for specialist workouts – the first time she'd got on a plane since she left hospital.

Despite these heroic efforts, her world championship debut didn't quite go to plan when, during four weeks of intense training in Northern Italy, Sam put so much strain on her body that she fractured her seventh rib, directly under her left scapula, robbing her left stroke of power, speed and control. But Sam, being Sam, simply would not give up. Despite this painful injury she gamely lined up for her qualifying heat in Milan, against the toughest competition she'd ever faced, and fought her way through to the next round. But bad luck struck again in the semi-final when a steering mishap, caused by floating weed fouling her rudder, sent Sam off-course and she was disqualified.

Though disappointed to bow out in such a fashion, my amazing wife finished her very first international sporting campaign ranked twelfth in the world. Better still, and despite being injured, she lopped three seconds off her previous personal best time during training, showing she has both the ability and the will to go even faster.

Even as her fractured rib was still healing, Sam set her sights on the 2016 Canoe Sprint World Cup in Germany. If she continues to improve she may even secure a place in the Australian Paralympic Team bound for Brazil in 2016. It's astonishing how far she's come in such a short time.

Penguin decided to stay in her favourite frangipani tree in Sydney, but Rueben, Noah, Oli and I travelled to Milan to watch Sam compete, after which we all boarded the train to Rome, Sam's favourite city, for a long overdue family holiday. Here we revisited the special places Sam and I first saw as young lovers – the Colosseum, Piazza Navona and the Spanish Steps – though now we enjoyed seeing all these through the eyes of our children, something we couldn't have even imagined fifteen years earlier.

Our European escape was very special for all of us, bringing back a great many happy memories and also, if I'm honest, a few sad ones. A freak accident meant that our Thai family vacation ended in tears, but our Italian family holiday began and ended with extremely loud cheers. Watching Sam conquer her disability and take on the world has been an absolutely thrilling experience for the entire Bloom family. She has survived the worst and gone on to achieve great things and, in doing so, she represents the best of us. It goes without saying that the boys and I are incredibly proud of our Sam but, more than that, we are so grateful to share each day with her and we love her dearly.

~

Over the last two years Penguin has grown up to be an independent young lady herself. Her glossy feathers and shiny beak have turned quite a few eligible magpie heads, though I don't believe she is ready to settle down just yet.

We love hearing her merry song whenever she drops by for a visit – bouncing into the kitchen, living room, bathroom or bedroom as if she owns the place – but now she spends more and more time away from our yard as she makes new friends and scouts out a territory that is all her own.

Penguin is very much a girl about town these days and sometimes she'll surprise Newport Beach locals by coming up to say a cheery sing-song hello to people enjoying coffee outside the café, buying a magazine at the newsagent or picking up items from the drycleaner – the world is her earthworm.

On one occasion I received a breathless phone call from a teacher at the nearby kindergarten that our three boys once attended, letting me know that Penguin had generously flown in to help the small children eat their lunches and asking me if I could please come and collect her as soon as possible. Our cheeky bird was delighted when I appeared, though she was a little nonplussed when she realised we weren't going to stay and enjoy the fabulous feast that had clearly been laid out for her by little pink fingers much like those she grew up with.

It was a joy to watch her fledge and take wing with such confidence. The most satisfying aspect of raising Penguin, however, has been seeing the kind of bird she turned out to be. She doesn't sit on the edge of life, she dives right in. She is clever, she is strong, she is resilient and she is bold. She is also mischievous, curious, and very funny.

Our little avian girl never looks for the worst in people; she is almost always upbeat and finds joy easily. Despite being a hunter by nature, and wise to the cruelty of her wild world, she welcomes everyone as a friend.

Penguin is also compassionate and surprisingly gentle – something we witnessed first-hand when she helped us care for other orphaned baby birds.

Sam and I both believe Penguin will make a wonderful mother one day but, for now, we are simply grateful that she's happy, healthy and completely free.

The endless blue sky was not ours to give, it is hers by right.

Wherever Penguin goes she will always be a part of us.

A personal message from
Sam Bloom

If you or someone close to you has suffered a serious spinal cord injury and been paralysed, then please know that what I now share with you is brutally honest. You deserve the truth and I promise you nothing else. I cannot pretend that I'm happy with how things have turned out. I'm not. But that doesn't mean I'm not a happy person, or that I'm not glad I'm still alive. I have enjoyed a great many things since my accident and I believe there are better days ahead. That said, I don't want to gloss over what has been and continues to be a great and terrible hardship.

Without the love and support of my husband and our children, our immediate families and our dearest friends (especially Penguin), I'm not sure I would still be here, and I know I wouldn't be doing as well as I am. Words can't express how grateful I am for their love, or how much I love them in return.

My accident has cast my entire life in sharp relief. I now realise that no one had ever said anything truly hurtful to me until I was told I would never walk again. In that sense, at least, I have been blessed. I am also fortunate, courtesy of my head injury, not to have any recollection of my fall or its immediate aftermath, so I have not had to relive that horror again and again.

My disability has made me aware of a level of suffering that was unknown to me and, while I would not wish this knowledge upon anyone, it has made me mindful of how much compassion is sorely needed in this world. In a strange way my accident has made me realise how lucky I really am – it has given me the chance to see the very best in my husband and our children, even while I was at my lowest point. These are beautiful insights for which I am grateful, despite their appalling cost.

Being paralysed is a little like waking up from a coma to find you are 120 years old. Your family and friends want you to be happy that you are still alive, but everything you do is very slow and very painful, and so much of what you enjoyed most, the things that actually made you feel alive, are now quite impossible. Perhaps if I was actually 120 years old a lifetime of happy memories might sustain me, but I am young, and I had every reason to believe that the bulk of my life adventure was still before me. There is so much I want to do, so many plans, so many dreams that now lie in pieces at my feet. My numb and useless feet.

Becoming a paraplegic has not been an unexpected gift; the new perspectives granted me cannot be equated with a great spiritual awakening and I don't feel this experience has made me a better person or given me newfound purpose. There have been many occasions when I have felt so bitter about the bizarre accident that left me like this that I wanted to vanish into the wilderness and scream my lungs out. These days I don't have nearly as many dark moments, but I still have them.

To those reading this who are just beginning a nightmare process of recovery and rehabilitation like that which I have been through, I know there is little I can say that will mean very much to you right now. I was so consumed with anger and regret after my accident that almost nothing positive got through to me. I was certain I would never smile or laugh ever again but thankfully, in the end, I was proved wrong.

I don't pretend to know everything about spinal cord injury, and I appreciate that everyone's situation is unique. But I can tell you that the icy cold fear in your heart that you will always be a freak, that the best of your life is over and that the real you is gone forever ... that's all normal. The thoughts of suicide and wishing you were dead – that's normal too.

There was a long spell when I nursed an irrational hatred for almost everyone and everything related to my paralysis. I was angry with the entire nation of Thailand, so much so that I couldn't even stomach the red curry with beef from our local Thai takeaway that was once one of my favourite things. It sounds crazy, I know – but pain, regret, grief and frustration make you a little crazy.

Likewise there will be a period when almost anything anyone says or does will make you feel incredibly sad or angry or both. For a while I became toxically jealous of everybody who continued to lead a normal life; watching girls running down to the beach with surfboards under their arms would reduce me to a puddle of angry tears. I knew it made no sense and wasn't remotely healthy, but I still felt this way.

Talking through what you are feeling can be helpful, if you can bring yourself to talk about such things. After a glass of wine I can be quite chatty but I am naturally very quiet, so I found that keeping a private diary of my highs and lows was a good way to put things in context and deconstruct my negative feelings. But though this was helpful, I found that nothing is better than saying things out loud. There's just something about putting your fear and your anger into words that robs these horrible feelings of their power over you.

In this regard, Penguin was a wonderful sounding board for me. Penguin always listened attentively without becoming visibly upset and never accidentally said anything thoughtless in response. My swearing might have made the angels blush, but I was able to vent all my frustrations and spit out all the vicious, ugly things that were eating away at me and know that I was harming no one. Flushing the emotional venom out of my system helped me feel better and put me in a far more positive mood around the many wonderful people who were doing their very best to help me.

Of course, not everyone has a bird like Penguin, and there is a limit to what one can communicate to people who have not experienced what you and I are now forced to endure. Many intelligent and compassionate people you love and admire have no idea what being paralysed means – they assume that being confined to a wheelchair is as comfortable as can be. They cannot comprehend the constant pain, hopelessness and humiliation that are an everyday, every hour, every minute reality. Don't be angry with them, it's not their fault – no one talks about this stuff.

It's in your best interests to seek out and follow the best medical advice. But that is still not enough. The scope and rate of your recovery is entirely your responsibility. You have to tackle your symptoms and limitations on your own terms, and the harder you work at this, the better you will feel. There is no magic bullet, no miracle and no shortcut.

Despite the devastating physical nature of our injuries, the battle going on inside your head is the hardest to overcome. When it comes to making positive progress following spinal injury I believe eighty per cent is mental and twenty per cent is physical. Anything you can do to improve your attitude will help you move beyond being a depressed blob rolling around in a wheelchair. Conversely, anything that sets you back mentally can quickly halt your progress and even send you backwards.

A few fundamental things have helped me the most since leaving hospital. The first is having a supportive inner circle, by which I mean your immediate family and your closest friends. My inner circle was just my husband and our children, my mum and my sister. That's all. Over time I began to include some close friends, but I kept it small.

It may seem counterintuitive, in terms of getting the support you need, but do not feel obliged to let all your friends and acquaintances in while you are navigating the earliest part of your recovery. If you're not careful you can be trampled by a herd of weepy well-wishers. Definitely try to stay clear of people who feel it is their job to say vapid, cheery things and repeatedly call you an 'inspiration' – they will quickly drive you insane and leave you feeling exhausted, angry and withdrawn.

Let friends know that you are grateful for their kindness but right now you need personal space to focus on coming to terms with your new life. If they insist on helping, give them simple tasks: picking up the shopping, taking your kids to soccer practice or baking a casserole – something practical that makes family life a little easier and helps maintain the connection with those you care about without depleting your energy reserves. When the time is right you will be ready to reconnect with close friends, and all those who are true friends will understand and respect this.

One of the most difficult things for me to overcome was my acute embarrassment. It may sound ridiculous but it's true. I hated looking strange, I hated not being able to dress how I used to dress, I hated thinking old friends were judging me or pitying me or comparing me to my former self. There were occasions where I felt disgusting – like Death in drag. I also constantly worried that, having no urinary sensation whatsoever and having also lost my sense of smell, I might have wet myself and not even known about it.

Initially I found it far easier to make new friends or be around complete strangers, people who only knew me as I am now, not as I was. This may seem a pathetic cop-out, but it highlights our basic desire to be treated normally. Some well-meaning friends cannot help but look at you as if you are a broken child who needs babysitting. Nor can they resist trying to cheer you up by prattling on about shared experiences from the good old days before your accident, which can be deeply upsetting.

It's easy to become withdrawn when you are in pain;

your self-esteem has been shattered and your mobility is reduced to almost nothing. But while I needed more personal space than most people realised, I also learned that getting out and about was essential to being happy and making meaningful progress. You certainly don't have to be paralysed to become a self-obsessed bore, but it helps. Even though it's far harder to get out and experience interesting things than it used to be, this is something that I wished I had pursued earlier. I urge you to do the same.

Looking back I now realise that socialising became easier about two years after my accident. It was no coincidence. By then I was committed to competitive kayaking and I had something to feel excited about and look forward to. I didn't realise this at the time but kayaking gave me back a great deal of my self-confidence and was the key to having something fresh and fun to talk about. This in turn added a positive dimension to all of my social interactions and expanded my circle of good friends.

Another fundamental that helped me was basic physical strength and fitness. It sounds obvious but early on all I could think about was the physical function I had lost, and how hard everything seemed. Over time I began to appreciate that increasing my physical strength and endurance distracted me from the constant pain I felt and also made everyday tasks easier, which in turn gave me more energy to commit to new and more interesting challenges. Not having the muscle to power your wheelchair over a wet towel your kids have left in the hallway is a sure way to feel feeble and pathetic. So believe me when I say that anything you can do to improve your functional flexibility, mobility, strength and coordination will prevent you from wasting time, effort and tears on petty domestic endeavours. You have far better things to do.

Of course training for a purpose beyond beating your disability is better still. And this is where sport and friendly competition come into play. I was always athletic and so the transition to competitive sport post-accident wasn't a great leap for me. But even if you are not naturally a sporty person I encourage you to seek out a physical challenge that compels you to train regularly in a way that produces measurable results. Having simple goals to aim for at each session – such as lifting a little more weight, achieving one additional repetition, greater distance or a slightly faster time – is very helpful when it comes to staying motivated.

Regardless of the physical activity you choose, it won't come easy at first. It took me at least two months just to be able to sit in a kayak without tipping myself into the water, which was initially terrifying as I was securely strapped into my seat with a heavy-duty Velcro belt and I feared it might be difficult to escape if I capsized (it actually wasn't hard at all).

I didn't take up kayaking with competition in mind – I just wanted to be out on the water. I loved getting out of the house, I craved the physical release, I enjoyed finessing my technique and going faster and, over time, I gradually improved to the point where new opportunities presented themselves. I don't want to suggest that kayaking is my new reason for living – it's not; my family are still the centre of my universe. But paddling has become an important part of my life and, when I consider how far I've come since I first got home from hospital, I am very grateful that I gave it a go and that I stuck with it.

Of course, any activity you enjoy doing is good for you, and the more effort and concentration it involves the better. Boredom is our number-one enemy – when your mind has nothing to do but focus on your discomfort and how angry you are about what has happened to you, then it can become terribly destructive. The pain starts to feel worse and your depression grows. Being paralysed is tough enough on you and your family and friends without your becoming bitter – so if it takes a little sweat and a few blisters to feel better in the long run, then it's certainly worth it.

You never know how your desires and appetites will change after your accident. I'm still drawn to the sea; I guess I'm just a water baby at heart. When I first got back in the ocean I thought it would feel wonderful, but it didn't. Even small waves overwhelmed me and I felt like I had a metal corset around my chest; breathing was difficult and quite frightening. However, over time, I have rediscovered the joys of swimming – I'm not the most graceful frog in the pond, and I haven't yet mastered diving underwater, but I enjoy the exercise and the strange yet refreshing sensation of waterborne weightlessness.

Despite my sense of taste being drastically reduced, I still enjoy cooking and baking, though it took a while to remaster my recipes, during which time I dished up quite a few disasters. Call me old-fashioned, but it feels very special to do traditional, motherly things for my family, especially those little treats that make them happy – I'm pleased to say my dad's apricot slice still gets appreciative smiles from my four men.

The key to beating boredom and making your new world bigger is to try as many new things as you can, and to accept that some will be wonderful and some a disaster, and to be okay with either outcome. You cannot know what you are good at or what you might enjoy until you try it a few times, so I encourage you to say yes a lot more than no, and to persist even when something doesn't feel quite right at first.

One measure of your recovery will be the degree to which you can take on responsibilities beyond merely looking after yourself. Caring for Penguin when she was a sickly little chick was incredibly rewarding for me. Helping her regain her strength and independence helped me enormously on so many levels. As often as I am able, I try to put myself in a position where people rely on me and not the other way around. It could be as simple as making dinner or driving someone where they need to go. It's not easy, but it does happen more and more, and when such opportunities arise they reaffirm that I have something to contribute to those around me, that I am in control of my life and therefore I can make a difference.

Life will never be as it was before your accident, and this is not easy for you or anyone else in our situation to accept. Then again, it's not easy for me to accept that Rod Stewart has sold over a hundred million records, but there it is. Striving against our limitations is part of what it means to be alive. You and I are not the first people on earth to become paralysed and nor will we be the last. Others have gone on to live stimulating and rewarding lives and we can too. Others have also had complete emotional meltdowns from time to time, and we'll probably suffer our fair share of those as well.

The truth is that in some ways you are not the same person you were. More than half of your body is now just coming along for the ride. I have often felt like two-thirds of me has died, and I suspect I'll always have a small storm cloud of sadness and anger lurking over my shoulder. But so long as you have choices, then you are still your own person. No one can expect every day to be perfect, but don't give yourself extra cause for regret by living in the past and thereby quitting on your present and your future. It's up to you to choose how you will face the challenges and hard times ahead, and how you will seize the opportunities for creativity, productivity and happiness.

To the family and close friends of someone who has recently been paralysed, I am sorry for the sadness and hopelessness you are feeling. I know that when someone close to you suffers a severe spinal injury their intimate circle also struggles with the pain and uncertainty of their situation. Your sense of loss is real, and you need to process this as best you can – don't be afraid to seek help from someone who has been through this.

If you want to be supportive, the first step is never to get caught feeling sorry for yourself or wishing things could be like they were before your loved one's injury. However sad and upset you feel about what has happened, it's nothing compared to how they are feeling. That said, your workload just tripled and your personal time has been cut in half. Also you now have to be brave and positive around someone who is angry, in terrible pain and deeply depressed. It's no picnic.

All I can tell you is to try to communicate normally – do your best to look past the wheelchair to the person you've always known and loved. Speak to that person and not the invalid sitting in front of you. Be sensitive to our limitations; don't rub salt into our wounds by talking about things we are currently prevented from enjoying. In time this won't be such an issue, but the first year or so is especially hard. Please don't tell us horror stories about people who have it worse than we do and try to demonstrate how lucky we are. And don't overuse extreme examples of disabled people conquering impossible challenges such as climbing Mount Everest using only their pinkie fingers, as if that is what we should be aiming for. A little extra encouragement is great, but right now our personal Mount Everest is a lot closer to home.

The worst time for us is when we first get out of the hospital. There's an awful moment where the sugary excitement of coming home crumbles to dust when we realise that our cherished sanctuary looks and feels completely different to us from a wheelchair. While stuck in the spinal ward we dream about being back in our own bed, but without all the medical amenities everything is far more difficult at home than we'd imagined. Also, for the first time in many months, we're now the only paralysed person in the building. The presence of our fellow spinal-injury patients was strangely reassuring, but now it's just us stuck in a wheelchair while everyone else goes on with life more or less as they always have. Not being able to undertake our old routine results in a horrible sense of dislocation from a life we loved. Watching my husband pick up the slack, and in effect become a single parent for our three boys, made me feel as if I wasn't a real mother or even part of the family any more.

Don't expect us to know everything about our condition, or to be able to communicate this. Do your own research, find out as much as you can so that you better understand what we are going through. Instead of feeling helpless, try to find ways to make a meaningful difference. My husband, Cameron, spent a lot of time online looking for better options for medical treatment and resources. Among other things, he tracked down a newfangled German catheter valve that was vastly superior to the ones I had been using and also a cheap, second-hand wheelchair that I could roll into the saltwater at the beach – not exactly the sexiest presents, but they made a very positive impression. Cameron organised a fundraising event that enabled us to buy a modified car that I could drive with my hands, and also made it possible for us to remodel the bathroom and the kitchen to accommodate my wheelchair. His incredible efforts not only made me feel very loved, but made a real and immediate difference to my quality of life, which in turn improved life for our whole family. He would be embarrassed if I called him my hero, but I do think he is totally awesome.

Always remember that there is more than one person to look after. We have you, but who do you have? We're not able to look after your needs and feelings while we are struggling to cope with our disability, so you must make time for yourself and continue to live a rich, full life in order to stay healthy and happy, for everyone's sake. You need to get out of the house, interact with friends and do things that refresh your body and spirit after a tough day. You are our able-bodied ambassador to the rest of the world, and if you bring back interesting stories and ideas, special treats, kind wishes and an upbeat mindset, then you've done a terrific job.

Distractions are great, so be creative – try to suggest new things and be ready to deliver a little extra push to help get us moving. And by all means pursue new interests yourself – who knows, something that you take up might be a conduit for us both finding something new we love to do. Cameron and the boys got into beekeeping last summer, which was a little weird (especially as Cameron is highly allergic to bees) but also quite wonderful. I wasn't sure I'd have much of a hands-on role in managing the beehives but I enjoyed the happy drama of it all from day one. When it came time to harvest the honey I was surprised and delighted by how much I could do to help. We all took turns in spinning the frames of honey and I was able to do much of the labelling and bottling with the boys. We then expanded our venture by creating organic lip balm and surfboard wax from the honeycomb, and the boys sold these as well as the jars of delicious organic honey to earn extra pocket money. Not in a million years would I have thought of beekeeping as something I would enjoy, but Cameron's curiosity delivered a marvellous learning experience for our children and provided great fun for all of us. In fact, bottling our first jars of 'Bungan Honey' was probably the first truly happy family memory we created since my accident.

Above all, I encourage you not to feel hurt when you get caught in the crossfire of us raging against life, the universe and everything. It's not about you, honestly; we're simply upset about what has happened to us and how little we can change our situation. We miss our old life. We miss our old selves. We regret all the little decisions and random events that led to us being injured. We hate having wheels for legs and we just want things to go back to how they were, and sometimes this longing seems beyond human endurance. The reality is that we can't get through this without you, and yet there are times when we hate that this is true. It's a difficult balance between genuine gratitude and profound despair. We may never be able to fully acknowledge the depth of our pain or how much we appreciate your help, but just remember that your love keeps us alive.

I am not at peace with my condition – I absolutely detest being paralysed and I cringe whenever I hear the word 'disabled'. I would give almost anything to stand on my own two feet again. I don't need to go dancing, or climb a mountain, or win an Olympic gold medal – just to walk down the beach holding my husband's hand and feeling the wet sand between my toes once more would be enough.

But whatever the pain and the regret, I know that every day I can share with my family is a gift. Every day presents an opportunity to watch my beautiful boys grow into young men, and for me to grow as a person. And every day brings new hope for a cure.

To be in the twenty-first century and not have found a cure for spinal cord injury is painfully astonishing. There are almost ninety million people living with spinal cord injury in the world today, and up to five hundred thousand new cases are reported every single year (mostly young men, just entering their prime). According to the World Health Organization, most of these people, like myself, will have a greatly reduced life expectancy, and are also five times more likely to commit suicide, especially during the first year after their accident.

Thankfully some of the brightest minds in medical science are starting to make real progress in the repair and regeneration of severed and badly damaged nerves as a result of spinal cord injury. Innovative techniques such as spinal cord implants, cell transplants, electro-acupuncture and the advent of epidural spinal stimulators give me great hope that one day I might have feeling and function in my torso and legs again. That one day I might fully regain my independence.

This once seemingly impossible dream is getting closer and closer. However, the realisation of this important medical goal is entirely dependent on the financial support needed to fund ground-breaking research.

I'm proud to say that my husband, Cameron Bloom, and our friend Bradley Trevor Greive are each donating 10 per cent of their book royalties from the sale of *Penguin Bloom* to support the vital work currently underway at Wings for Life UK. Their generous charitable contribution is also being matched by our publisher, Canongate, which I think is an extraordinary gesture.

If reading our story has touched you then I sincerely hope you will consider making a donation to Wings for Life UK via their official website: www.wingsforlife.com.

Penguin helped save my life, but your support will help get me back on my feet.

With love and sincere gratitude,

Sam Bloom

We support

WINGS for LIFE

SPINAL CORD RESEARCH FOUNDATION.

New day.
New possibilities.

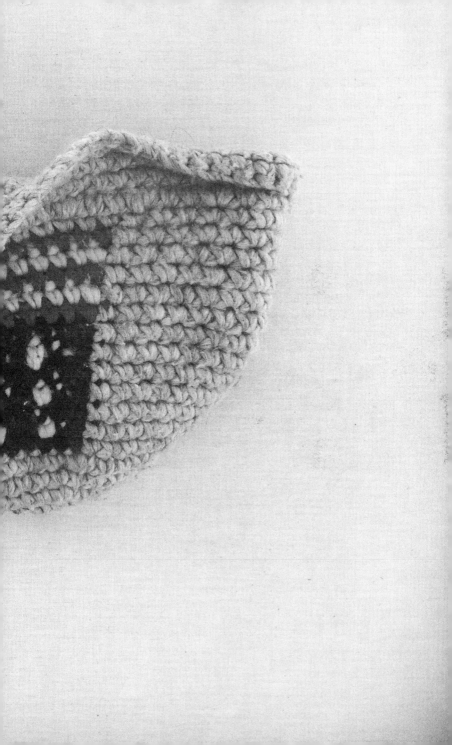